J
372.889
Mo     Moncure, Jane Belk
      Our Thanksgiving book. Illustrated by Mina
   Gow McLean.   Elgin,Ill., The Child's World,
   [1976.]
      unp.   col.illus.

12,136

      1.Thanksgiving Day.   2.Schools-Exercises and
   recreations.   I.McLean,Mina Gow,illus.   II.Title.

# Our Thanksgiving Book

By Jane Belk Moncure
Illustrated by
Mina Gow McLean

THE CHILD'S WORLD

ELGIN, ILLINOIS 60120

This is a book about how we celebrated
Thanksgiving in our class. You will have more ideas
in your class.

Library of Congress Cataloging in Publication Data

Moncure, Jane Belk.
    Our Thanksgiving book)

    (A Special day book)
    SUMMARY: A group of children and their
teacher discover many ways in which they can
celebrate Thanksgiving Day.
    1. Thanksgiving Day—Juvenile literature.
2. Schools—Exercises and recreations—Juvenile
literature 1. Thanksgiving Day I. McLean,
Mina. II. Title.
GT4975.M66        372.8'8'9        76-10997
ISBN 0-913778-41-9

Distributed by Childrens Press, 1224 West Van Buren Street, Chicago,
Illinois 60607

One day Miss Berry brought a real ship model to school. "This is a model of a ship called the *Mayflower*," she said. "Does anyone know who sailed to America on this ship?"

"The Pilgrims!" said Julie.

"Was the real *Mayflower* a big ship?" asked Tina.

"It was big enough to hold more than a hundred people," said Miss Berry.

"We could build a ship big enough to hold our whole class," said Jason.

While some children built the ship out of blocks, others made Pilgrim hats and bonnets.

Miss Berry helped Jane paint the word, *Mayflower,* on a flag. Jane and Julie climbed aboard.

Matthew waved to them. "I am an Indian," he said. "Pilgrims, I welcome you to America."

MAYFLOWER

staple

staple

The next day, Matthew brought a big box of real Indian things to school. With it was a letter from Matthew's mother. Here is what it said.

Dear Friends,

Matthew's daddy was in a Makowaian Indian tribe when he was a boy.

These hawk feathers were used for dancing.

The beaded headband was given him by a Sioux Indian chief.

The children may wear the moccasins and play the drum.

Keep this collection until Thanksgiving.

Love,
Mrs. Darrah

Everyone wanted to be an Indian like Matthew.

Douglas brought chicken feathers from his farm to use in making Indian headbands for the class.

"First, you must do a good deed," said Matthew. "Then you can stick a feather in the back of your headband."

"I took the dishes off the table," said Elizabeth.

"I fed my dog," said Caroline.

"The Indians helped the Pilgrims. That was a very good deed," said Matthew.

"We can be thankful for the Indians," said Miss Berry. "They gave the Pilgrims corn to eat the first cold winter they were here."

The next day, Miss Berry brought a basket of dried corn to school. "Corn was a great gift the Indians gave the Pilgrims," she said. "Each of you may have an ear of corn to husk."

"This is like peeling a banana!" said Van.

"This is fun," said Jennie. "I have lots of corn seeds in my plate."

"How did the Indians make cornbread?" asked Caroline.

"First they mashed the corn into cornmeal. We can do that, too," said Miss Berry. "We must take the corn outside."

Miss Berry found some flat rocks. She showed the children how to mash the corn between the rocks.

"How did they cook it?" asked Julie.

"They mixed the cornmeal with water and made little cakes, like pancakes. Then they cooked the cornmeal cakes on hot rocks over a fire. We can make uncooked cornmeal cakes for the birds today," Miss Berry said.

Soon children were scattering cornmeal cakes in the field by the playground.

"Happy Thanksgiving, birds," said Tina.

"Did the Indian and Pilgrim children have toys?" asked Danielle.

"Yes, they did," said Miss Berry. "I will make an Indian toy for you." She taped some chicken feathers around the end of a corn cob.

"That looks like a fat arrow," said Jody.

"It is a toy dart," said Miss Berry.

"We can make some, too," said Jody.

Then Miss Berry folded some corn husks together. She shaped arms and taped them, then taped the body. She painted a face on one side.

"You are making a little doll," said Danielle. "We can make some, too."

corn cob dart

corn husk doll

tape

Karen found a paper cup on the art shelf. "I can make an Indian puppet," she said. She turned the cup upside down and drew a face on it. Then she made a little headband and taped it around her puppet.

Alice made a Pilgrim puppet with a tall black hat.

"Let's have a puppet show," said Karen. So they did.

"Hello, Pilgrim," said Karen's puppet. "Why are you wearing that funny black hat?"

"Hello, Indian," answered Alice's puppet. "Why are you wearing that funny feather hat?"

"Let's trade hats and be friends," they both said.

"The Pilgrims and Indians were friends that first Thanksgiving," said Miss Berry. "We still think of friends at Thanksgiving time."

"My Papa and Nana sent me a Thanksgiving card," said Jennie.

"Let's make some Thanksgiving cards for our families," said Miss Berry. "What will we need?"

"Colored paper."

"Scissors and paste."

"Crayons."

Soon the children were making lovely Thanksgiving cards in many different shapes and colors.

"The Pilgrims and Indians were friends that first Thanksgiving," said Miss Berry. "We still think of friends at Thanksgiving time."

"My Papa and Nana sent me a Thanksgiving card," said Jennie.

"Let's make some Thanksgiving cards for our families," said Miss Berry. "What will we need?"

"Colored paper."

"Scissors and paste."

"Crayons."

Soon the children were making lovely Thanksgiving cards in many different shapes and colors.

Jason traced his hand on a piece of paper. "Look!" he said. "I can make a little turkey with my hand print."

Steve traced his hand another way. "Look!" he said. "I can make an Indian with my hand print."

Jane traced her hand still another way. "I think I can make a Pilgrim with my hand print," she said.

Jason's turkey

Steve's Indian

Jane's hand was closed
when she traced it.

One day it rained very hard. Matthew, Jason, and Van were building with blocks.

"If we were Indians out hunting, we would build a shelter," said Matthew.

"There is a roll of brown paper in the art room," said Miss Berry.

"Let's build a lean-to," said Matthew.

Miss Berry cut long strips of brown paper and put them on the floor. The children decorated the papers with Indian designs. When the sheets were dry, Miss Berry stapled one end of each sheet to the bulletin board. She taped the other end of each to some heavy blocks.

"This is neat!" said Scott.

The children crawled inside to play.

"Thanksgiving really means giving thanks," said Miss Berry. "The Pilgrims came to America so they could worship God in their own special way. Their first winter here was very hard. They were hungry and sick and, oh, so cold. Some of them even died. But spring came, and the Pilgrims planted crops. When fall came, they harvested their crops. They were thankful for a good crop of corn. They were thankful for the Indians who had helped them. So the Pilgrims gave a Thanksgiving party and invited their Indian friends.

"Tomorrow we will have a Thanksgiving party. We need lots of turkeys for our tables."

Miss Berry showed the children how to stuff paper bags with newspaper and turn them into fat Thanksgiving turkeys.

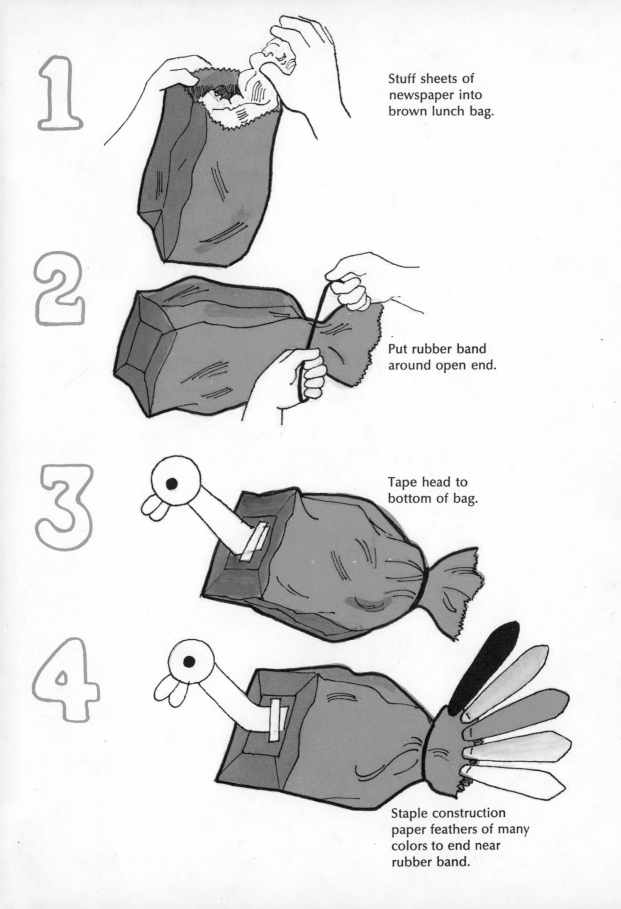

**1** Stuff sheets of newspaper into brown lunch bag.

**2** Put rubber band around open end.

**3** Tape head to bottom of bag.

**4** Staple construction paper feathers of many colors to end near rubber band.

The next day, at the party, the children played "Pin the Feathers on the Turkey." The turkey was so funny, everybody laughed.

Then the children played "The Pilgrims on the *Mayflower*," singing new words to "The Farmer in the Dell." The Pilgrim took a wife; the wife took a child; the child took a cat; the cat took a mouse; and the mouse took the cheese.

"Now, everyone, sit on the rug," said Miss Berry. "In a few minutes we will have hot cornbread to eat. We need something to put on our cornbread, something that is almost the color of cheese."

Miss Berry held up a jar of cream. "Can you guess what this will be?"

No one knew.

"Let's find out," she said. She passed the jar of thick cream around the circle, singing,

"Shake, shake, shake,
What will we make?"

Everyone shook the jar of cream many times.

"Shake, shake, shake!"

"I see butter!" shouted Elizabeth.

Just then, in came Caroline's mother, dressed as a Pilgrim, with a basket of cornbread.

Next, in came Jeff's mother, dressed as a Pilgrim, with a basket of popcorn.

And then, in came Matthew's mother, dressed as an Indian, with a basket of apples.

"Welcome," said all the children. They sat down at a very long table. Nuts and raisins were in little paper cups beside each plate.

"This is like the real Thanksgiving," said Matthew. "If I had been there long ago, I'd have been one of the Indians the Pilgrims invited."